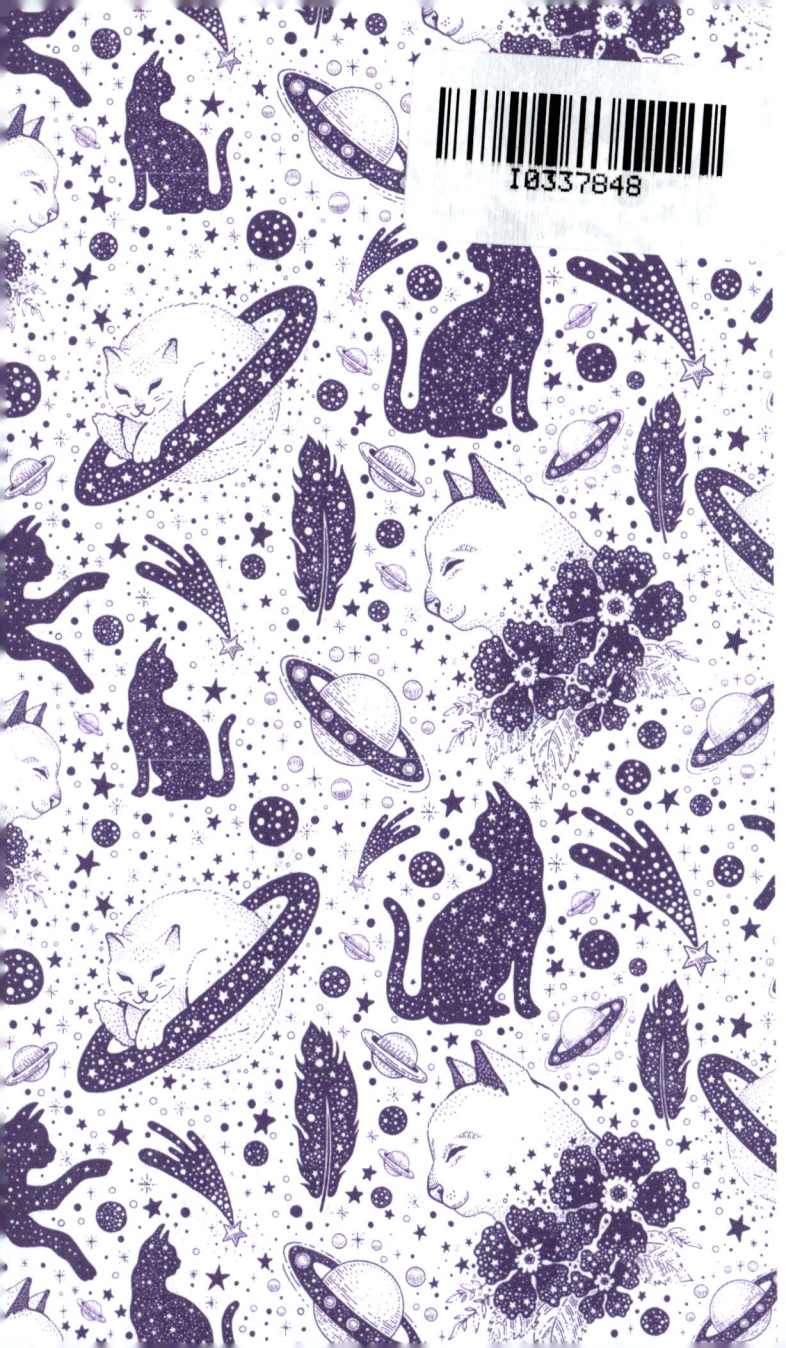

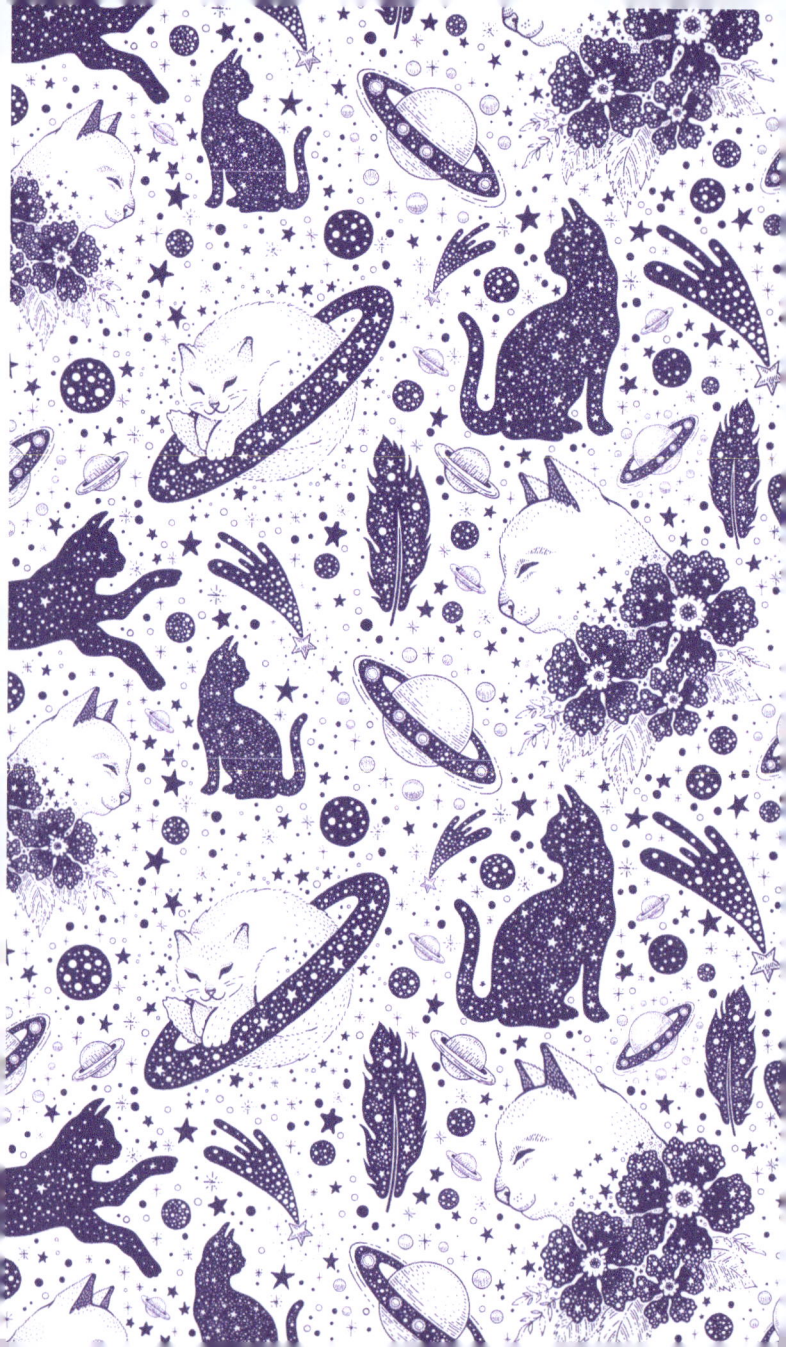

Amanda Clarke is a devoted seeker of magic, wisdom, and the profound mysteries that connect us to the universe. Amanda has woven her passion for cats and her fascination with the mystical arts into the enchanting tapestry of "Divine Guidance: Mystic Tarot Cat."

Having spent many years immersed in the world of Tarot and Meditation, Amanda sought to create a divination tool that goes beyond the traditional and ventures into the realm of playful spirituality.

"Divine Guidance: Mystic Tarot Cat" is a testament to Amanda's creative vision, a vision that bridges the mystical with the earthly, and invites readers to embark on a journey of self-discovery through the captivating wisdom of the cat spirits.

As an advocate for spiritual exploration and the healing power of the animal-human connection, Amanda Clarke invites you to join her in unlocking the secrets of the universe with the delightful and insightful pages of "Divine Guidance: Mystic Tarot Cat."

Also by Amanda Clarke
More on the Bookshelves at
www.korupublishing.com

Daily Wisdom
ORACLE OF THE TAROT CAT
Cat Spirit Daily Insights

Amanda M Clarke

Second Edition

Experience the Stunning Beauty of Daily Wisdom: Oracle of the Tarot Cat. Let yourself be carried into a realm of enchantment where all 78 Tarot Cats have been reimagined. Witness captivating illustrations that bring the cards to life. Indulge in the visual splendor of this exquisitely illustrated book and enhance your divination journey to a whole new level.

Copyright © 2024 by Koru Lifestylist

All rights reserved. All content, materials, and intellectual property in this book or any other platform owned by Koru Lifestylist are protected by copyright laws. This includes text, images, graphics, videos, audio, software, and any other form of content that may be produced by Koru Lifestylist.

No part of this content may be reproduced, distributed, or transmitted in any form or by any means without the prior written permission of Koru Lifestylist. This means that you cannot copy, reproduce, or use any of the content in this book for commercial or personal purposes without the express written consent of Koru Lifestylist.

Unauthorized use of any copyrighted material owned by Koru Lifestylist may result in legal action being taken against you. Koru Lifestylist reserves the right to pursue all available legal remedies against any individual or entity found to be infringing on its copyright.

In summary, Koru Lifestylist © 2024 holds exclusive rights to all the content produced by it, and any unauthorized use of such content will result in legal action.

Dear Seekers of Secrets,

Step into the wondrous realm of "Oracle of the Tarot Cat," where magic and mystery intertwine. As the weaver of this mystical tapestry, my heart brims with delight in revealing the essence and enchantment poured into every fiber of this creation.

With each stroke of my pen, I endeavored to imbue these pages with a harmonious blend of wonder, elegance, and spiritual resonance. Here, the ancient language of Tarot entwines with the mischievous yet profound spirit of our feline companions. I bid you to delve deep into this oracle, engage the spirits of the cats with your inquiries, and behold the metamorphic energies awaiting your embrace.

In the soft whispers of gratitude, I extend my thanks to the beloved community of cat aficionados, the devotees of Tarot's enigma, and all who cherish the dance between the ethereal and the earthly. Your unwavering support has been the celestial beacon guiding the manifestation of this oracle, a gift I humbly present to you.

May "Oracle of the Tarot Cat" illuminate your path with insight, illumination, and the purring magic of revelation.

Embracing you with love and feline enchantment,

Amanda Clarke

Disclaimer: This Oracle of the Cat Tarot book provides information on spiritual readings and interpretation, but it is not intended as a substitute for professional advice, diagnosis, or treatment. The information contained in this book is provided for educational and entertainment purposes only and is not meant to be taken as specific advice for individual circumstances. The author and publisher make no representations or warranties with respect to the accuracy or completeness of the contents of this book and specifically disclaim any implied warranties of merchantability or fitness for a particular purpose. The reader should always consult with a licensed professional for any specific concerns or questions. The author and publisher shall not be liable for any loss or damage caused or alleged to have been caused, directly or indirectly, by the information contained in this book. The use of this book is at the reader's sole risk

Why a book?

You are a mystical feline, and in the ethereal realm, a multitude of guardian spirits surrounds you, purring words of affectionate and insightful guidance. Ever-present, they lead you towards a path of contentment, well-being, and love. Communicating through enigmatic codes, varied voices, and symbolic gestures, their messages may elude your immediate understanding.

Cat Tarot proves to be a remarkably potent and secure practice, fostering healing by dispelling fears and emotional barriers. It unveils the purpose of your feline existence and offers profound responses to your innermost queries. The angels, archangels, or spirit guides, depending on your chosen deity, encircle you, governed by the universal Law of Free Will, abiding by the principle that their intervention requires your consent.

Many feline enthusiasts turn to Tarot Cards to unravel the secrets of cat-centric divination. I crafted Oracle of a Tarot Cat pocket-book for its simplicity, speed, and user-friendly approach. Portable and convenient in size, it becomes your companion, allowing swift readings whenever you find yourself lost in contemplation, facing decisions, or grappling with uncertainties throughout your day. With this handy book which easily fits into your bag, backpack or purse, you'll shed anxieties, soothe your mind, and experience physical vitality, empowering you to navigate each day with courage and a clear feline consciousness.

Using the Book

Step 1: CLEAR YOUR BOOKS ENERGY

Since your book is a sensitive instrument and has been through many hands to reach you, you will need to clear it of any energy it may have absorbed. Steps One and Two only need to be completed every so often when the energies of the book become clogged.

It is a good idea to ground yourself first before clearing the book. Do this by sitting on a standard kitchen chair, with your feet comfortably flat on the floor. You can do this with shoes on, but it is better in bare feet. Better still, stand barefoot on the ground in the open, this will ensure all energies will be fully grounded out into the nothingness of the earth.

Hold the book in the palm of your non-dominant hand as this is the hand that receives energy.

Form a fist with your other hand and knock on the book once with your fist sending all energies from the book to the ground and into nothingness.

This clears out the old energy and the book is now blank and is ready to be imbued with your energy.

Step 2: CONSECRATE THE BOOK

Flip through the pages of the book ensuring you touch every page with your thumb, fingers or hand. This will start infusing it with your energy.

Hold the book in your dominant hand up to your heart and

think about the prayers or intentions you would like to infuse the book with. For example, you may say to yourself in your minds-eye or out aloud: -

"Oh majestic feline spirits, grant me accuracy and specificity in our readings, showering blessings on all involved. Guide me to stay connected to my higher self, attuning my senses to hear, see, feel, and know the sacred messages flowing through these pages. In reverence, I seek your divine guidance."

After this step, you may wish to keep your book wrapped in a silk scarf or special bag to keep other people's energies from transferring to your pages.

Step 3: PERFORMING A READING

In your mind think of your question as you flip through the book. You may flip backward and forward until you feel the sense to stop. By the laws of the mystical feline powers, you will ALWAYS land on the page devoted purrrely for you at your present moment. So, if whilst pawing through these pages you have a feeling of stopping... then stop!

You may close your eyes and take a deep breath. Count to 5 as you exhale long and slow. Open your eyes and read the page your hand rests on.

Read slowly the words the realm of the cat guides have chosen for you. Pay close attention to our thoughts and feelings as you read the words. All senses play a part in your reading. The 'Mantra' is designed to keep you focused throughout the day, to keep you on your feet, on your path.

JOURNAL PAGES
Each page for your readings comes with its own special journal page! It's a purrfect spot for you to jot down your thoughts, how you're feeling, or what's going on while you're reading. Don't forget to mark the date and scribble a little sentence—it'll be like leaving a paw print in your own magical book of moments!

The Answers You Seek

Are Within

The purr-fect card selected by the Cat Spirits for your daily reading today...

The Devil

Temptation dances in playful shadows, freedom found in releasing bonds. I break free with a playful spirit. My mantra:
'In playful liberation, I find freedom.'

Behold, the card selected by the Cat Spirits for your daily reading today.

The Hermit

Solitude embraced with a playful spirit, wisdom gleaned from quiet contemplation. I seek enlightenment with a curious heart.

My mantra: 'In playful solitude, I find wisdom.'

The feline forces have aligned to present this perfect card for your daily reading...

Ace of Wands

New adventures beckon, playful fires ignite within. I seize each opportunity with a playful spirit, knowing that creativity fuels my joy.

My mantra: 'With each leap, I embrace new adventures.'

Witness the card handpicked by the Cat Spirits for your daily reading today..

Ten of Pentacles

Harmony thrives in playful togetherness, family bonds are my treasure. Joy resides in shared moments, love and unity are our legacy.

My mantra: 'In playful unity, our family thrives.'

Behold, the card selected by the Cat Spirits for your daily reading today...

Eight of Wands

Rapid movements lead to discovery, adventures soar with playful speed. I embrace change with a playful spirit. My mantra: 'In playful motion, I find exploration.'

The meow-nificent card chosen by the Cat Spirits for your daily guidance...

The Emperor

Authority in playful wisdom, guidance rooted in gentle strength. I lead with playful authority, fostering balance for all.

My mantra: 'With playful guidance, I bring harmony.'

Today's chosen card is a gift from the Cat Spirits for your daily guidance…

Three of Swords

Wounds heal with playful love, tears fade amidst cuddles.
Comfort and joy reside within mended hearts.
My mantra:
'Through playful comfort, I find healing.'

Today's chosen card is a gift from the Cat Spirits for your daily guidance...

Knight of Swords

Swift and clever, I prowl the realms of intellect, cutting through confusion with sharp precision. Clarity is my ally, and mysteries unravel in my keen gaze.

Mantra: 'Swift mind, clarity cuts through confusion.'

The Cat Spirits bring forth this purr-fect card for your daily reading today...

Four of Cups

Treasures are around, if only seen with playful eyes. I seek joy in the familiar, finding hidden delights.

My mantra:

'Through playful eyes, I discover hidden treasures.'

This perfectly chosen card is from the wisdom of the Cat Spirits for your daily guidance..

Death

Transformation whispers, endings bring playful beginnings.
I embrace change with a kitten's curiosity.
My mantra:
'In playful transitions, I find renewal.'

This perfectly chosen card is from the wisdom of the feline spirits for your daily reading......

Eight of Pentacles

Craftsmanship brings joy, playful learning leads to mastery.
Each effort is a step toward perfection.
My mantra:
'In playful dedication, I craft my purr-fect world.'

Witness the perfect card chosen by the Cat Spirits for your daily reading...

The Sun

Radiance beams in playful warmth, joy thrives in every sunny moment. I embrace happiness with a playful spirit.

My mantra:

'With every ray, I find joy.'

Today's card is a selection from the Cat Spirits for your daily guidance..

Five of Wands

Skirmishes lead to growth, unity thrives amidst playful challenges. Harmony emerges from playful conflicts.
My mantra:
'In playful balance, we find strength.'

The Cat Spirits have revealed this ideal card for your daily reading today...

Seven of Cups

Dreams twirl, fantasies bloom. I seek clarity amidst playful wishes, focusing on realistic aspirations.

My mantra:

'With playful focus, I seek my dreams.'

The feline forces have aligned to present this perfect card for your daily reading.....

Temperance

Balance blooms in playful harmony, moderation whispers in every step. I seek equilibrium with a playful heart.

My mantra:

'With playful balance, I find harmony.'

*The Cat Spirits have revealed this ideal card
for your daily reading today....*

The High Priestess

Intuition guides with a purr, secrets revealed through playful whispers. I embrace inner wisdom with a kitten's curiosity.

My mantra:

'In playful silence, I find wisdom.'

Today's reading is handpicked by the Cat Spirits, presenting this perfect card…

The Moon

Mystery weaves in playful shadows, intuition guides through playful illusions. I seek truth with a curious heart.

My mantra:

'In playful exploration, I find clarity'

Today's guidance is from the Cat Spirits, revealing this perfect card...

Ace of Swords

Clarity reigns, my thoughts are playful swords. I embrace truth with a playful heart, sharpening my mind like claws.

My mantra:

'With each leap, I seek clarity.'

Behold, the purr-fect card chosen by the Cat Spirits for your daily reading...

Six of Cups

Nostalgia whispers, past joys linger. I cherish playful innocence, relishing sweet memories.

My mantra:
'In playful moments, nostalgia brings warmth'.

Witness the perfect card chosen by the Cat Spirits for your daily reading...

Page of Swords

Curiosity fuels my quest for knowledge. I explore with a playful heart, learning from every adventure.

My mantra:

'With playful curiosity, I seek wisdom.'

Today's chosen card is a gift from the Cat Spirits for your daily guidance...

Page of Pentacles

Curiosity fuels my learning, knowledge is my playful adventure. I embrace wisdom with wide-eyed wonder.

My mantra:

'With playful curiosity, I explore the world.'

Today's reading is guided by the Cat Spirits, revealing this perfect card...

Two of Wands

Choices whisper, horizons call. I trust my playful instincts, seeking balance in playful decisions.

My mantra:

'In playful harmony, I find my path forward.'

Behold, the card selected by the Cat Spirits for your daily reading today...

Seven of Wands

Defend playfully, courage thrives amidst challenges. I stand firm with a playful heart, embracing resilience.

My mantra:

'With playful courage, I overcome obstacles.'

This chosen card is a message from the Cat Spirits for your daily guidance...

Ten of Wands

Lessons hide in burdens, strength in playful perseverance. I carry my load, learning from each playful step.

My mantra:

'In playful lessons, I find growth.'

The Cat Spirits bring forth this perfect card for your daily reading today…

King of Pentacles

Wisdom grounds my leadership, authority is guided by playful insight. Stability and prosperity flourish through understanding.

My mantra: 'With playful wisdom, I lead to prosperity.'

The feline forces have aligned to present this ideal card for your daily reading…

Wheel of Fortune

Destiny spins playfully, cycles dance in eternal motions. I embrace change with a playful soul.

My mantra:

'With every turn, I find opportunity.

The Cat Spirits have aligned to present this ideal card for your daily reading today…

Six of Wands

Victory sings in playful achievements, success in every playful step. I embrace triumph with a playful heart.

My mantra:

'With every leap, I celebrate success.'

Behold, the card selected by the Cat Spirits for your daily reading today.

Eight of Swords

Tangled in worries, freedom's a playful leap away. I untangle doubts, embracing playful liberation.
My mantra:
'In playful freedom, I find courage.'

This card, selected by the Cat Spirits, is your guide for today's reading...

Ten of Swords

Lessons hide amidst playful defeats, guiding wisdom in each tumble. I rise, wiser from playful struggles.

My mantra:

'In playful lessons, I find strength.'

*Today's guidance is from the Cat Spirits,
presenting this perfect card...*

Strength

Courage in playful whispers, resilience in every gentle touch.
I face challenges with a playful heart.
My mantra:
'In playful bravery, I find strength.'

Behold, the card selected by the Cat Spirits for your daily reading today...

Ace of Cups

Love and joy overflow, my heart is a playful fountain. I embrace emotions with playful curiosity, knowing that happiness surrounds me.

My mantra: 'With every purr, I embrace love and joy.'

*Witness the card handpicked by the Cat Spirits
for your daily reading today…*

Queen of Cups

Nurturing warmth radiates, compassion guides every action.
I lead with love, fostering emotional understanding.
My mantra:
'With every purr, I nurture love.'

*The Cat Spirits have pawed this perfect card
for your daily reading today…*

Seven of Swords

Honesty triumphs over mischief, truth echoes louder than
tricks. Kindness prevails in genuine friendships.

My mantra:

'With playful honesty, I find trust.'

Witness the perfect card selected by the Cat Spirits for your daily reading...

Nine of Swords

Midnight fears fade with dawn's playful light. Cuddles soothe fretful hearts, fears melt away.
My mantra:
'With each playful dawn, fears disappear.'

Witness the card handpicked by the Cat Spirits for your daily reading today…

Five of Swords

Mock battles, yet unity thrives. Harmony dances amidst playful skirmishes.

My mantra:

'In playful balance, we find unity.'

This card, selected by the Cat Spirits, is your guide for today's reading...

The Tower

Disruption sparks playful change, foundations crumble for new beginnings. I embrace transformation with a kitten's resilience.

My mantra: 'In playful upheaval, I find renewal.'

The Cat Spirits have aligned to present this ideal card for your daily reading today...

Three of Pentacles

Together, we create wonders through playful teamwork.
Collaboration is our joyful melody.
My mantra:
'In playful unity, we craft beautiful achievements.'

Today's card is a selection from the Cat Spirits for your daily guidance...

Four of Pentacles

Generosity fills my heart, releasing abundance through playful sharing. Joy blossoms when I share my treasures.

My mantra:

'By sharing joyously, I invite abundance.'

The Cat Spirits reveal this ideal card for your daily reading today...

Queen of Swords

Kindness sharpens insight, leading with a playful intellect. I nurture creativity with gentle authority.

My mantra:

'With playful guidance, I foster wisdom.'

The Cat Spirits present this perfectly chosen card for your daily reading...

The Empress

Nurturing warmth blooms, abundance thrives in playful care. I lead with love and a playful heart.
My mantra:
'With each purr, I nurture growth.'

Today's card is a selection from the Cat Spirits for your daily guidance...

Eight of Cups

Wanderlust whispers, adventures await. I seek comfort but embrace playful exploration beyond familiar puddles.

My mantra:

'In playful discovery, I find my path.'

Today's card is a selection from the Cat Spirits for your daily guidance...

Queen of Pentacles

Nurturing care radiates warmth, abundance flows through playful guidance. I lead with love, fostering prosperity for all.

My mantra: 'With playful care, I nurture abundance.'

The Cat Spirits reveal this ideal card for your daily reading today...

Judgement

Rebirth whispers in playful echoes, lessons learned through playful reflections. I embrace transformation with a curious heart.

My mantra: 'In playful renewal, I find wisdom.'

The chosen card, a divine message from the Cat Spirits for your daily reading…

The Lovers

Harmony sings in playful unity, connections thrive in loving bonds. I embrace relationships with a playful soul.

My mantra:

'In playful togetherness, love blossoms.'

The Cat Spirits bring forth this purr-fect card for your daily reading today…

The World

Completion sings in playful cycles, unity dances in every connection. I celebrate wholeness with a playful soul.

My mantra:

'With playful harmony, I embrace completeness.'

The Cat Spirits have gifted this ideal card for your daily reading today...

The Star

Hope twinkles in playful dreams, guidance found in starry whispers. I embrace optimism with a playful soul.
My mantra:
'With playful hope, I find guidance.'

The whiskered messengers have selected this ideal card for your daily reading today...

The Hanged Man

Surrender found in playful pause, enlightenment blooms in letting go. I learn through playful release.

My mantra:

'With playful surrender, I find enlightenment.'

Witness the chosen card, a gift from the Cat Spirits for your daily reading…

Nine of Wands

Resilience purrs in every struggle, fortitude amidst playful battles. I stand strong, knowing playfulness fuels my endurance.

My mantra:

'With playful strength, I overcome challenges.'

This perfectly chosen card is from the wisdom of the Cat Spirits for your daily guidance...

Three of Cups

Laughter dances, celebrations bloom. Joyous gatherings create playful memories.

My mantra:

'In shared joy, our happiness multiplies.'

Behold, the card handpicked by the Cat Spirits for your daily guidance....

King of Cups

Emotional balance shapes my wisdom, empathy guides my authority. I lead with a playful heart, nurturing understanding in others.

My mantra: 'With playful wisdom, I guide with empathy.'

This perfectly chosen card is from the wisdom of the feline spirits for your daily reading...

Nine of Cups

Contentment purrs within, wishes granted. I embrace gratitude for my blessings.

My mantra:

'With every purr, I embrace fulfilled wishes.'

The Cat Spirits have gifted this ideal card for your daily reading today....

Nine of Pentacles

Independence brings contentment, my sanctuary is within. I revel in my playful solitude, surrounded by abundant joy.

My mantra:

'In playful self-sufficiency, I find happiness.'

This paw-some card is the selection of the Cat Spirits for your daily reading.....

The Chariot

Direction found in playful determination, victories won with a kitten's resolve. I move forward with playful strength.

My mantra:

'With playful determination, I conquer.'

Here's the card hand-delivered by the Cat Spirits for your daily reading....

Four of Wands

Celebrate joyously, harmony echoes in playful gatherings.
Shared moments create lasting happiness.
My mantra:
'In playful unity, our happiness blossoms.'

The feline forces have aligned to present this ideal card for your daily reading…

King of Swords

Mentor's wisdom guides with playful authority. I lead with gentle encouragement, nurturing creativity in others.
My mantra:
'With playful wisdom, I lead with understanding.'

HeadingHere ..

Five of Cups

Tears dry, but lessons linger. I embrace sadness with a
playful heart, learning from sorrows.
My mantra:
'Through playful learning, I find healing.'

This card is a divine offering from the Cat Spirits for your daily guidance....

Ace of Swords

Clarity reigns, my thoughts are playful swords. I embrace truth with a playful heart, sharpening my mind like claws.
My mantra:
'With each leap, I seek clarity.'

This card is a divine offering from the Cat Spirits for your daily guidance…

Ace of Pentacles

Playfulness leads to abundance, treasures await my curious paws. I embrace each opportunity, knowing that prosperity surround me.

My mantra

'With playful curiosity, I welcome abundance into my life.'

The Cat Spirits bring forth this perfect card for your daily reading today…

Six of Swords

Adventure whispers, horizons beckon. I trust the journey, exploring with playful curiosity.

My mantra:

'In playful exploration, I find new horizons.'"

Today's card is handpicked by the Cat Spirits, offering their guidance...

Ten of Cups

Harmony purrs in cozy nests, love is our playful legacy. Joy thrives in shared moments, unity is our treasure.

My mantra:

'In playful togetherness, our happiness blossoms.'

This perfectly chosen card is from the wisdom of the feline spirits for your daily reading......

Knight of Cups

A dreamy cat, I embrace love's whispers, navigating the emotional seas with grace. My heart's melody guides me, weaving tales of joy and compassion.

My Mantra: 'Love's flow, my heart guides gracefully.'

Today's card is a selection from the Cat Spirits for your daily guidance...

Seven of Pentacles

Patience guides my dreams, growth is a playful journey.
Each step is a playful paw toward fruitful abundance.
My mantra:
'With patient playfulness, my dreams blossom.'

The Cats wish for you to have chosen this card for today's reading....

The Magician

Magic whispers in playful gestures, creativity sparks in every move. I wield my powers with a playful heart.
My mantra:
'With playful creativity, I manifest dreams.'"

The Cat Spirits have aligned to present this ideal card for your daily reading today...

Page of Wands

Curiosity sparks playful exploration, seeking knowledge with a kitten's wonder. I learn from every adventure with a playful heart.

My mantra: 'With playful curiosity, I seek wisdom.'

Today's reading is guided by the Cat Spirits, revealing this perfect card...

Queen of Wands

Warmth radiates in playful leadership, creativity fuels my guidance. I lead with passion and a playful heart.
My mantra:
'With playful guidance, I nurture creativity.'

Behold, the card handpicked by the Cat Spirits for your daily guidance...

Justice

Fairness guides with playful balance, decisions made with a kind heart. I seek equality with a playful spirit.

My mantra:

'In playful fairness, I find justice.'

*Today's reading is guided by the Cat Spirits,
revealing this perfect card…*

The Fool

In playful curiosity, I dance on new paths, embracing each adventure with a kitten's spirit.

My mantra:

'With every leap, I welcome new beginnings.'

The chosen card, a divine message from the Cat Spirits for your daily reading...

Five of Pentacles

Unity is our strength in moments of scarcity, love is our true wealth. Together, we overcome challenges with joy.

My mantra:

'In playful unity, we find warmth and richness.'"

Today's card is handpicked by the Cat Spirits, offering their guidance...

Six of Pentacles

Generosity is my nature, each act of giving a joyous gift.
The dance of sharing brings happiness.
My mantra:
'In playful giving and receiving, I find abundance.'

The purr-fect card selected by the Cat Spirits for your daily reading today.

King of Wands

Authority tempered with playfulness, wisdom in every decision. I lead with a playful spirit, fostering creativity in all endeavors.

My mantra: 'With playful wisdom, I guide with passion.'

The Cat Spirits have pawed this perfect card for your daily reading today...

Two of Pentacles

Balance is my dance, adapting with playful ease. Life's changes bring joyous challenges.

My mantra:

'In playful balance, I find harmony amidst life's waves.'

*Today's guidance is from the Cat Spirits,
revealing this perfect card…*

The Hierophant

Tradition guides with a playful ritual, wisdom echoed in every lesson. I honor knowledge with a playful heart.
My mantra:
'In playful learning, I find wisdom.'

The Cat Spirits have ordained this card for your daily reading today...

Three of Wands

Exploration fuels my dreams, horizons await playful discovery. I embrace the journey, seeking adventure with a wide-eyed wonder.

My mantra: 'With each step, I explore new horizons.'

The Cat Spirits reveal this ideal card for your daily reading today...

Two of Cups

Friendship's harmony sings, our bond is a playful melody.
Together, we find joy in each other.
My mantra:
'In playful unity, our friendship thrives.'

The Cat Spirits have ordained this card for your daily reading today…

Knight of Wands

A fiery feline spirit, I dance with passion and adventure, leaving pawprints of courage on life's wild canvas. Dreams soar high and wide in the vibrant flames of my pursuit. My Mantra: 'Passion's dance, courage leaves pawprints.'

The Cat Spirits bring forth this ideal card for your daily guidance today....

Four of Swords

Rest is a playful respite, dreams sparkle under cozy blankets.
Recharge to frolic anew in renewed vigor.
My mantra:
'In playful rest, I find rejuvenation.'

Witness the card handpicked by the Cat Spirits for your daily reading today....

Two of Swords

Choices linger, uncertainty whispers. I trust my playful instincts, finding balance between heart and mind.

My mantra:

'In playful harmony, I find my path.'

This card, chosen by the Cat Spirits, is a divine message for your guidance....

Page of Cups

Curiosity sparks, learning becomes a playful adventure. I explore emotions with a wide-eyed wonder.

My mantra:

'With playful curiosity, I learn.'

Today's card is a selection from the Cat Spirits for your daily guidance…

Knight of Pentacles

Paws firmly grounded on Earth, embody patience and prosperity. With purpose you sow seeds of abundance. My Mantra: 'Grounded strength, patience blooms abundance'

My Journaling Pages

My daily thoughts....

My daily thoughts....

My daily thoughts....

My daily thoughts....

My daily thoughts....

My daily thoughts....

My daily thoughts....

My daily thoughts....

My daily thoughts....

My daily thoughts....

My daily thoughts....

My daily thoughts....

My daily thoughts....

My daily thoughts....

My daily thoughts....

My daily thoughts....

My daily thoughts....

My daily thoughts....

My daily thoughts....

My daily thoughts....

My daily thoughts....

My daily thoughts....

My daily thoughts....

My daily thoughts....

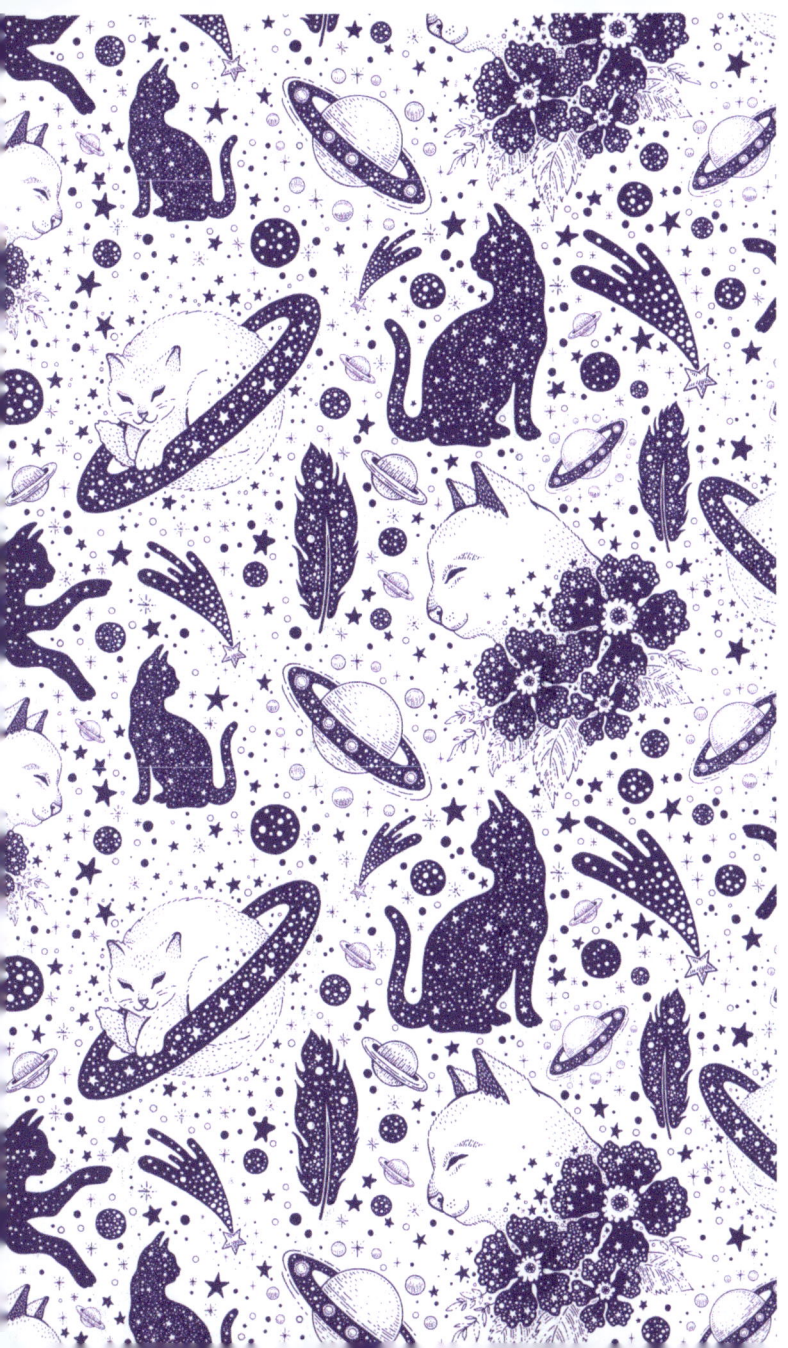

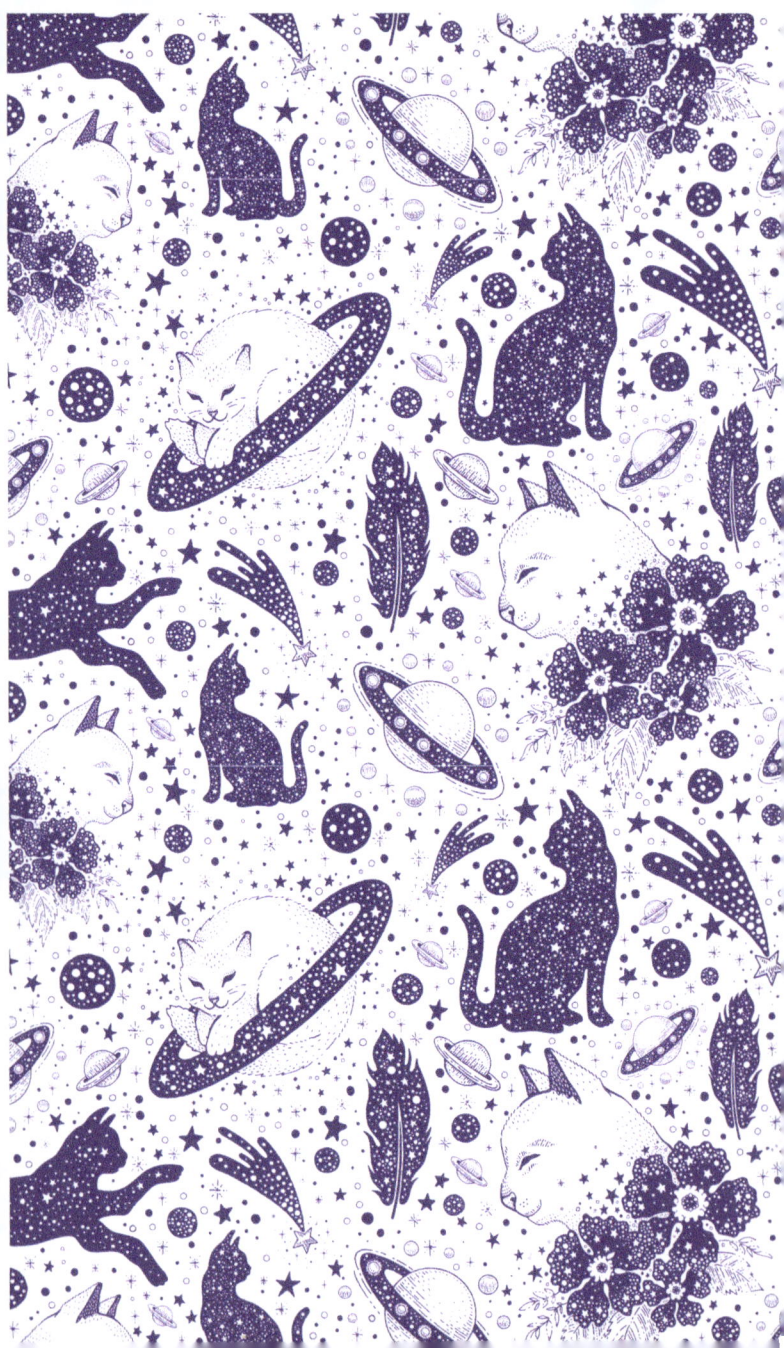

www.ingramcontent.com/pod-product-compliance
Lightning Source LLC
Chambersburg PA
CBHW062034290426
44109CB00026B/2624